The United Nations
Leadership and Challenges in a Global World

The UN Security Council
and the Center of Power

The United Nations:
Leadership and Challenges in a Global World

The United Nations
Leadership and Challenges in a Global World

The UN Security Council and the Center of Power

Ida Walker

SERIES ADVISOR
Bruce Russett

Mason Crest Publishers
Philadelphia

Mason Crest
450 Parkway Drive, Suite D
Broomall, PA 19008
www.masoncrest.com

Printed and bound in the United States of America.

First printing
9 8 7 6 5 4 3 2 1

Series ISBN: 978-1-4222-3427-3
ISBN: 978-1-4222-3436-5
ebook ISBN: 978-1-4222-8550-3

Library of Congress Cataloging-in-Publication Data
on file

Design by Sherry Williams and Tilman Reitzle, Oxygen Design Group.
Cover photos: Fotolia/Nobilior (top); Corel (bottom).

CONTENTS

KEY ICONS TO LOOK FOR:

Words to Understand: These words with their easy-to-understand definitions will increase the reader's understanding of the text, while building vocabulary skills.

Sidebars: This boxed material within the main text allows readers to build knowledge, gain insights, explore possibilities, and broaden their perspectives by weaving together additional information to provide realistic and holistic perspectives.

Research Projects: Readers are pointed toward areas of further inquiry connected to each chapter. Suggestions are provided for projects that encourage deeper research and analysis.

Text-Dependent Questions: These questions send the reader back to the text for more careful attention to the evidence presented there.

Series Glossary of Key Terms: This back-of-the-book glossary contains terminology used throughout the series. Words found here increase the reader's ability to read and comprehend higher-level books and articles in this field.

INTRODUCTION

by Dr. Bruce Russett

T HE UNITED NATIONS WAS FOUNDED IN 1945 by the victors of World War II. They hoped the new organization could learn from the mistakes of the League of Nations that followed World War I—and prevent another war.

The United Nations has not been able to bring worldwide peace; that would be an unrealistic hope. But it has contributed in important ways to the world's experience of more than sixty years without a new world war. Despite its flaws, the United Nations has contributed to peace.

Like any big organization, the United Nations is composed of many separate units with different jobs. These units make three different kinds of contributions. The most obvious to students in North America and other democracies are those that can have a direct and immediate impact for peace.

Especially prominent is the Security Council, which is the only UN unit that can authorize the use of military force against countries and can require all UN members to cooperate in isolating an aggressor country's economy. In the Security Council, each of the big powers—Britain, China, France, Russia, and the United States—can veto any proposed action. That's because the founders of United Nations recognized that if the Council tried to take any military action against the strong opposition of a big power it would result in war. As a result, the United Nations was often sidelined during the Cold War era. Since the end of the Cold War in 1990, however, the Council has authorized many military actions, some directed against specific aggressors but most intended as more neutral peacekeeping efforts. Most of its peacekeeping efforts have been to end civil wars rather than wars between countries. Not all have succeeded, but many have. The United Nations Secretary-General also has had an important role in mediating some conflicts.

UN units that promote trade and economic development make a different kind of contribution. Some help to establish free markets for greater prosperity, or like the UN Development Programme, provide economic and technical assistance to reduce poverty in poor countries. Some are especially concerned with environmental problems or health issues. For example, the World Health Organization and UNICEF deserve great credit for eliminating the deadly disease of smallpox from the world. Poor countries especially support the United Nations for this reason. Since many wars, within and between countries, stem from economic deprivation, these efforts make an important indirect contribution to peace.

Still other units make a third contribution: they promote human rights. The High Commission for Refugees, for example, has worked to ease the distress of millions of refugees who have fled their countries to escape from war and political persecution. A special unit of the Secretary-General's office has supervised and assisted free elections in more than ninety countries. It tries to establish stable and democratic governments in newly independent countries or in countries where the people have defeated a dictatorial government. Other units promote the rights of women, children, and religious and ethnic minorities. The General Assembly provides a useful setting for debate on these and other issues.

These three kinds of action—to end violence, to reduce poverty, and to promote social and political justice—all make a contribution to peace. True peace requires all three, working together.

The UN does not always succeed: like individuals, it makes mistakes . . . and it often learns from its mistakes. Despite the United Nations' occasional stumbles, over the years it has grown and moved for-ward. These books will show you how.

The atom bombs dropped on Hiroshima and Nagasaki in Japan at the end of World War II—and their devastating impact—helped to motivate the international community to establish a permanent organization to maintain international security and peace.

CHAPTER ONE

The Evolution of the United Nations

Though 1945 brought the defeat of the **Axis powers** and the end of World War II, the world was far from a peaceful place. The **Allies** had proven they would use atomic weapons, and for many countries, that threat loomed large. Fortunately, the victors were no more interested in a continuing conflict than were the defeated powers. Three years previously—even before the end of the war—the leaders of twenty-six countries had met to devise a plan for maintaining peace in the world after the war ended. That meeting was the beginning of the United Nations.

 WORDS TO UNDERSTAND

Allies: the countries, including the United Kingdom, the United States, China, and the Soviet Union, that fought against the Axis powers in World War II.

Axis powers: the group of countries, including Germany, Italy, and Japan, that fought against the Allies in World War II.

delegates: individuals chosen to represent or act on behalf of another person, organization, or government.

preamble: the opening section of a document that explains the purpose of what follows.

The League of Nations

The desire for worldwide peace did not begin with World War II and its aftermath. After all, there had already been one global war, and its effects were long lasting. The twenty-six nations' leaders wanted a peacekeeping organization that would be more effective than its predecessor, the League of Nations.

As World War I was winding down, leaders of the soon-to-be victorious countries met to establish an organization that could prevent the devastation caused by history's first global war. Edward Grey, British foreign secretary (a position similar to that of the secretary of state in the United States), initially proposed the idea of such an organization. U.S. president Woodrow Wilson enthusiastically threw his support behind the creation of the League of Nations, making it part of his famous "Fourteen Points for Peace." He campaigned to include the formation of the League as part of the Treaty of Versailles, which would formally end World War I.

The creation of the League of Nations was part of President Woodrow Wilson's "Fourteen Points for Peace."

Despite the fact that its president was instrumental in establishing the League of Nations, the United States did not join the League. Nevertheless, the League met in London in January 1920 to ratify the Treaty of Versailles (also referred to as the Treaty of Trianon). In November of the same year, it met in Geneva, Switzerland, where it set up its headquarters.

For a variety of reasons, including the United States' nonparticipation, member countries' reluctance to enforce sanctions on countries that violated the League's policies, and its inability to prevent World War II, the League of Nations is considered a failure. However, it did increase the world's appetite for an organization with real peacekeeping powers.

Delegations from both sides in World War I emerge from the Trianon Palace at Versailles, France, in 1920 following the conclusion of negotiations, which led to the Treaty of Versailles.

The sculpture, *Non-Violence*, by Swedish artist Carl Fredrik Reuterswärd, located at the UN Plaza in New York City.

The Creation of the United Nations

Since the League of Nations failed to stop another global war, it was obvious to many world leaders that changes had to be made to create a viable peacekeeping organization. Initial steps toward that goal occurred in 1942. The term "United Nations" was used for the first time on January 1, 1942, in American president Franklin D. Roosevelt's Declaration by United Nations. This declaration was the promise by representatives of twenty-six nations to keep fighting until the members of the Axis powers finally admitted defeat. Unlike President Wilson and the League of Nations, President Roosevelt and this document had the support of the United States.

Between August and October of 1944, representatives from China, the Soviet Union, the United Kingdom, and the United States met at Dumbarton Oaks, a nineteenth-century mansion in Georgetown, Virginia, just outside Washington, D.C. There, they worked to develop the framework that would establish and govern the United Nations. In April 1945, fifty countries sent representatives to the United Nations Conference on International Organization in San Francisco. The **delegates** discussed the proposals formulated at Dumbarton Oaks and wrote the UN Charter. Representatives of the fifty countries signed the charter on June 26, 1945; representatives from Poland did not attend the conference, but signed the charter later and became one of the fifty-one original members of the United Nations.

When China, France, the Soviet Union, the United Kingdom, and the United States signed the charter on October 24, 1945, the United Nations was officially born. Those signatories continue to play an important role in the United Nations and its policies. They are the five permanent members of the Security Council, established by the UN Charter.

WHO OWNS THE UN?

Although the United Nations Headquarters is located in New York City, it is not owned by New York City, the state of New York, or even the United States. The building and the land on which it sits are in an international zone and owned by the members of the United Nations.

OFFICIAL LANGUAGES

The official languages of the United Nations, as established by its charter, are Chinese, English, French, Russian, and Spanish. Later, Arabic was added as an official language of the General Assembly, the Security Council, and the Economic and Social Council. European English spellings are traditionally used for international documents written in English. That is why they are used in the UN Charter although the United Nations is headquartered in the United States.

The UN Preamble

When the original UN membership—in effect, the first UN General Assembly—signed the charter, they established the principles under which the United Nations operates. The charter spells out the rights and obligations of its member states and puts in writing the principle prohibiting the use of force in any manner inconsistent with the founding purpose of the United Nations. The **preamble** of the charter states the goal of the United Nations to avoid another global conflict:

> We the Peoples of the United Nations Determined
>
> to save succeeding generations from the scourge of war, which twice in our lifetime has brought untold sorrow to mankind, and to reaffirm faith in fundamental human rights, in the dignity and worth of the human person, in the equal rights of men and women and of nations large and small, and to establish conditions under which justice and respect for the obligations arising from treaties and other sources of international law can be maintained, and to promote social progress and better standards of life in larger freedom,

The chamber where the Security Council meets at the United Nations headquarters in New York City viewed from the visitors section.

And for these Ends

to practice tolerance and live together in peace with one another as good neighbours, and to unite our strength to maintain international peace and security, and to ensure, by the acceptance of principles and the institution of methods, that armed force shall not be used, save in the common interest, and to employ international machinery for the promotion of the economic and social advancement of all peoples,

Have Resolved to Combine our Efforts to Accomplish these Aims. Accordingly, our respective Governments, through representatives assembled in the city of San Francisco, who have exhibited their full powers found to be in good and due form, have agreed to the present Charter of the United Nations and do hereby establish an international organization known as the United Nations.

One of the tools UN founders put in place to help it achieve these lofty goals was the Security Council.

CHAPTER ONE

TEXT-DEPENDENT QUESTIONS

1. When was the first time the term "United Nations" was used?

2. Who were the original signatories to the UN Charter?

3. What is the official language of the UN?

RESEARCH PROJECTS

1. Create a map showing the permanent and elected members of the Security Council.

2. Research and write a report about why the participation of the Soviet Union was so important to the creation of the United Nations and the Security Council.

British foreign secretary William Hague gives a speech at a UN Security Council Summit on September 23, 2010.

CHAPTER TWO

The Security Council and the UN Charter

The war-weary creators of the United Nations gave careful consideration to the establishment of the organ that would have the responsibility of maintaining world peace. Some people consider the Security Council the UN's most important department. Its creators knew it had to be strong, its role and principles firmly

 WORDS TO UNDERSTAND

arbitration: the process of resolving disputes through an impartial third party.

conciliation: action taken to reach agreement or settle a dispute and restore trust.

embargos: government restrictions on commerce, especially those that prohibit trade in a particular commodity or with a particular nation.

mediation: the intervention by a third party between two sides in a dispute to help them reach an agreement.

protocols: official ways of doing things.

established. The founders of the United Nations made certain that the roles and responsibilities of the Security Council were clearly stated in the UN Charter.

In general, the charter gives the Security Council the right to take action on any threat to world peace. The establishment and function of the Security Council are covered in Chapters V, VI, VII, VIII, and XII of the UN Charter. The primary responsibility of the council is to maintain world peace by diffusing conflicts and providing opposing parties an opportunity to settle conflicts nonviolently. Because of the importance of the Security Council, the countries represented on the council are chosen carefully, with many factors taken into consideration.

Under the Nuclear Non-Proliferation Treaty, only P-5 nations are allowed to have nuclear weapons.

Chapter V

Chapter V outlines the council's membership, functions and powers, voting, and procedures.

Membership on the Security Council

As a "reward" for their war efforts and for their work in establishing the United Nations, the Allied forces—China, France, the Russian Federation, the United Kingdom, and the United States—were given permanent seats on the Security Council. At first, the Security Council was limited to eleven members, including the five permanent members; they are sometimes referred to as the P-5. However, in 1965, Article 23 was amended to increase membership to fifteen. The remaining ten members are elected by the General Assembly to staggered two-year terms. When a country's name changed, such as occurred with the fall of the Soviet Union, the country is usually allowed to retain its seat on the Security Council under its new name.

Under the Nuclear Non-Proliferation Treaty, the P-5 are presently the only nations permitted to possess nuclear weapons. However, some non–P-5 countries, North Korea, India, Pakistan, and Israel for example, do have or are suspected of having nuclear weapons, despite the framework established by the UN Charter.

In 1963, it was decided that non-permanent membership should be geographically distributed: African and Asian states have five representatives, the Eastern European States have one, Latin American and Caribbean states are allocated two seats, and two come from Western European and other states.

> ## WHAT'S A STATE?
>
> In the United States, we're used to thinking of a state as something different from a country—so it may be confusing to read references to the "states" of Eastern Europe, Latin America, and elsewhere. According to Merriam Webster's dictionary, however, a state is any "politically organized body of people usually occupying a definite territory"—so the term applies to nations as well.

Functions and Powers of the Security Council

Chapter V, Article 24 states the Security Council's mission very clearly:

> 1. In order to ensure prompt and effective action by the United Nations, its Members confer on the Security Council primary responsibility for the maintenance of international peace and security, and agree that in carrying out its duties under this responsibility the Security Council acts on their behalf.

In summary, this means the General Assembly agrees to go along with whatever the Security Council decides to be the best action to take in its goal of maintaining world peace. This is a power unique to the Security Council. Other organs of the United Nations can make recommendations, but the Security Council makes policy.

Although the Security Council has a great deal of power, it must still act according to the principles of the United Nations as a peacekeeping organization. The specific powers of the council are covered in Chapters VI, VII, VIII, and XII of the charter and will be discussed later. The council is also required to keep the General Assembly informed of its practices and findings.

Voting

Each member on the Security Council has one vote, but the votes do not share equal power. For a vote on a procedural matter to pass, at least nine members must have voted in favor of passage. For a substantive matter to be passed—such as a decision to recommend sanctions be placed on a country—nine of the fifteen members must vote in its favor, but none of the P-5 can vote against the measure. This is often referred to as the veto power of the Security Council.

On March 5, 2014, the Security Council passed Resolution 2141 continuing the mandate of the expert panel reviewing the possibility of sanctions against North Korea for its nuclear weapons program. Pictured here is a military demonstration in 2010 in North Korea honoring the sixty-fifth anniversary of the country.

Veto power was agreed to at the Yalta Conference, held in 1945 in the Soviet Union, in order to convince the Soviet Union to join the United Nations. With that much power, it is no surprise that a long-running debate has occurred over expanding the number of permanent members.

Procedure

The world is a dynamic place, with many areas waiting for the next crisis to happen. Because of the need to act quickly, a Security Council member, but not necessarily one from the P-5, must always be at UN Headquarters in New York City. Meetings of the council can be held at UN Headquarters or wherever council membership thinks is appropriate.

The Security Council has complete freedom to determine its own procedures (as long as they don't violate UN standards), including the election of a president. The presidency of the council rotates among its members alphabetically according to the English spelling of the countries' names. Each president serves a one-month term.

The charter also gives the Security Council the right to create subsidiary organs it finds necessary to performing its mandate. Some of these include the Peacebuilding Commission, the Counter-Terrorism Committee, and the al Qaeda and Taliban Sanction Committee.

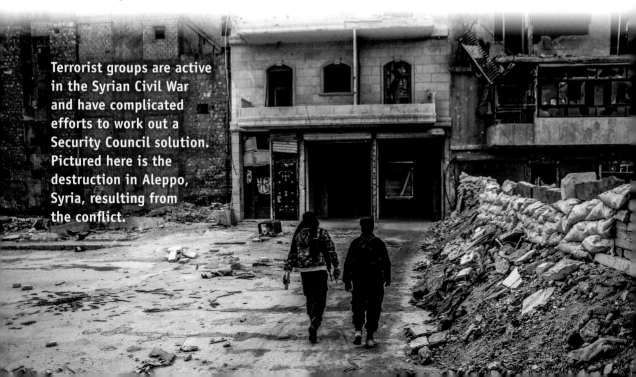

Terrorist groups are active in the Syrian Civil War and have complicated efforts to work out a Security Council solution. Pictured here is the destruction in Aleppo, Syria, resulting from the conflict.

THE FORMAT OF SECURITY COUNCIL RESOLUTIONS

Nearly all Security Council resolutions follow certain **protocols**. First of all, they reaffirm principles laid out in UN documents and/or recall previous resolutions on the same or similar matter. For instance, Resolution 2199 adopted by the Security Council on February 12, 2015, which condemns support of terrorist groups operating in Syria and Iraq, begins in this way:

The Security Council,

Reaffirming its primary responsibility for the maintenance of international peace and security, in accordance with the Charter of the United Nations,

Reaffirming that terrorism in all forms and manifestations constitutes one of the most serious threats to international peace and security and that any acts of terrorism are criminal and unjustifiable regardless of their motivations, whenever and by whomsoever committed, . . .

Resolutions frequently end with the same wording, which expresses the Security Council's commitment to address the issue under consideration. Indeed, Resolution 2199, in its final paragraph, states that the Security Council, "Decides to remain actively seized of the matter."

Chapter VI

The peaceful settlement of disputes is the subject of Chapter VI of the UN Charter. Maintaining world peace is, after all, the UN's primary goal.

According to the charter, the first step to conflict resolution is to attempt to find peaceful solutions through negotiation, **mediation**, **arbitration**, **conciliation**, and judicial settlement. If these methods fail, the conflicting countries should bring the matter to the Security Council.

The Security Council is also encouraged to investigate any situation it feels might lead to a dispute or to armed conflict. Other UN member states are allowed to bring such matters to the attention of the Security Council as well, even ones in which they are not directly involved. Countries that are not members of the United Nations can approach

THE TALIBAN

The Taliban is a fundamentalist Islamic group that once ruled in Afghanistan. When U.S. forces ousted them in reaction to the September 11, 2001, terrorist attacks in the United States, the Taliban went underground, fighting the U.S.-led coalition and continuing to sow terror in Afghan society.

The Security Council's work in maintaining pressure on terrorist and insurgent groups is geared toward the termination of violence and, hopefully, reconciliation as well. In this photo, former Taliban fighters turn their weapons over to the Afghan government in May 2012 and pledge their commitment to the Afghanistan Peace and Reintegration Program.

the Security Council or General Assembly in an attempt to avoid hostilities. There are strings attached, however; the petitioning country must agree in advance to the obligations necessary to a peaceful settlement.

At any point during its investigation, the Security Council can recommend settlement procedures to the opposing parties. The charter requires that the council take into consideration procedures the parties have already followed or are presently following. Generally, the Security Council recommends that the conflicting parties take all legal matters to the International Court of Justice.

Chapter VII

While the preceding chapters deal with peaceful settlements of international conflict, the UN Charter acknowledges that not all disagreements will be free of military intervention. Chapter VII explains the role of the Security Council in those cases.

The Security Council will always first encourage the conflicting bodies to solve their problems through such means as mediation. If that hasn't worked, the Security Council is authorized to make its own recommendations to solve the problem and maintain world peace, always remembering that maintaining peace is the primary goal of the UN Security Council. According to the charter, the recommendations made by the Security Council are "without prejudice to the rights, claims, or positions of the parties concerned."

Recommendations made by the Security Council wouldn't do much good if it didn't have a way to encourage disputing parties to accept them. Under Article 41, the Security Council has the responsibility to determine what measures can be put in place to "give teeth" to its recommendations. The use of armed forces is not considered at this point in conflict resolution. Economic sanctions such as **embargos**, interruption of means of transportation and communications, and the withdrawal of diplomats are examples of measures the Security Council might ask UN member states to approve.

Fortunately for the world, these peacekeeping methods sometimes work. However, not all conflicts are solved without the use of armed forces. Article 42 gives the Security Council the option of using air, sea, or land forces as necessary to keep or restore international peace. Generally, the Security Council will begin by sending in a peacekeeping force.

The use of the word "force" might lead some people to think that war is just around the corner once UN peacekeeping forces are sent to an area. That is not necessarily true; after all, the UN's emphasis is always on peacekeeping. A peacekeeping force is not sent into an area unless requested by the country in which it is stationed. Oftentimes, the UN Security Council will ask the opposing country or countries to agree to the placement of peacekeeping forces as well. UN peacekeeping forces perform many duties: police might be sent to maintain peace in an area

OTHER RESPONSIBILITIES OF THE SECURITY COUNCIL

The Security Council's work includes other tasks, some of which relate to more general UN matters. These include:

- recommending to the General Assembly the appointment of the secretary-general and, together with the Assembly, electing the Judges of the International Court of Justice;

- requesting the International Court of Justice to give an advisory opinion on any legal question;

- recommending to the General Assembly the admission of new members to the United Nations.

Article 42 of the UN Charter gives the Security Council the power to send troops where they are needed.

lacking public safety protection, civilians may be sent to monitor whether an election is conducted fairly, or military troops may be deployed to give a country's people a sense of safety. Although these troops are armed, they are ordered not to use their weapons except as a last resort in the case of self-defense.

Another method of encouraging conflicting countries to agree with Security Council recommendations is through the use of measures such as blockades. Blockades by armed forces operating on behalf of the United Nations are often used as a preliminary show of force; they show the countries involved that the United Nations and its Security Council mean business. Blockades encourage the conflicting countries to realize that the benefits they would receive by complying with recommendations far outweigh anything they could obtain by proceeding to armed conflict.

But sometimes, after all other options have been tried, the Security Council determines that force is needed. Article 43 describes the role of the member states in raising a peacekeeping force:

1. All Members of the United Nations, in order to contribute to the maintenance of international peace and security, undertake to make available to the Security Council, on its call and in accordance with a special agreement or agreements, armed forces, assistance, and facilities, including rights of passage, necessary for the purpose of maintaining international peace and security.

2. Such agreement or agreements shall govern the numbers and types of forces, their degree of readiness and general location, and the nature of the facilities and assistance to be provided.

3. The agreement or agreements shall be negotiated as soon as possible on the initiative of the Security Council. They shall be concluded between the Security Council and Members or between the Security Council and groups of Members and shall be subject to ratification by the signatory states in accordance with their respective constitutional processes.

The Security Council consults with all member states it asks to participate in peacekeeping operations.

The United States and UN Peacekeeping Missions

As a member of the United Nations and one of the P-5 on the Security Council, the United States participates in UN peacekeeping missions. However, its level of participation has been the source of much criticism. As of November 2014, 104,184 uniformed personnel had been serving UN peacekeepers. Of those, 37 troops, 90 civilian police, and 5 military experts were from the United States, one of the lowest contribution levels of any UN member state.

While U.S. forces are deployed with a UN mission, the president maintains control over them through his role as commander in chief. However, control is sometimes handed over to a trusted ally if it serves U.S. purposes.

A UN soldier from Sri Lanka assists U.S. Marine forces in distributing food to those affected by the 2010 earthquake in Haiti.

When planning the deployment of peacekeeping troops and other military requirements, the Military Staff Committee assists the Security Council. According to Article 47 of the charter, the Military Staff Committee is "responsible under the Security Council for the strategic direction of any armed forces placed at the disposal of the Security Council."

The Security Council recognizes that in the case of an attack, there's usually no time to follow the conflict resolution process it has established. It is also aware that a country's membership in the United Nations might make it more vulnerable to an attack by some countries. Article 51 reads:

> Nothing in the present Charter shall impair the inherent right of individual or collective self-defense if an armed attack occurs against a Member of the United Nations, until the Security Council has taken measures necessary to maintain international peace and security. Measures taken by Members in the exercise of this right of self-defense shall be immediately reported to the Security Council and shall not in any way affect the authority and responsibility of the Security Council under the present Charter to take at any time such action as it deems necessary in order to maintain or restore international peace and security.

This article allows the government of the country under attack to respond—but requires it to report to the Security Council about what actions it has taken.

* * *

With the admirable goal of maintaining world peace, one might think that an organization such as the Security Council would be free from criticism. Unfortunately, the power that comes with being a member of the council has brought it much criticism in primarily two areas—membership and transparency.

BLUE HELMETS

UN peacekeeping forces are often called "Blue Helmets" because of the bright blue helmets they wear. The UN has been conducting peacekeeping operations since 1948. As of February 2015, there are sixteen ongoing peacekeeping operations.

A UN peacekeeper from Uruguay guards a MONUSCO compound in Goma, in the Democratic Republic of the Congo, in June 2013.

CHAPTER TWO

TEXT-DEPENDENT QUESTIONS

1. Which countries have permanent seats on the Security Council?

2. Describe the theory behind the use of economic sanctions.

3. How many peacekeeping operations was the UN involved with in 2015?

RESEARCH PROJECTS

1. Research and create a photographic time line of one of the UN peacekeeping missions in 2014.

2. Divide into groups and debate whether the number of permanent members of the Security Council should be increased.

While the Security Council faces much criticism, the work of UN peacekeepers is often overlooked. Here peacekeepers from the UN Intervention Brigade ensure the protection of civilians in the territory of Rutshuru, Tanzania, in October 2013.

CHAPTER THREE

The Security Council's Critics

Membership on the UN Security Council is prized. No other UN organ has as much power as the Security Council, especially the P-5. Many other countries want to have a turn on the Security Council, and how membership is determined is one of the areas under much criticism.

 WORDS TO UNDERSTAND

agenda: the various matters that need to be dealt with at a given time.

decolonization: the process by which a colony is granted its independence.

globalization: the various processes that increase the connections between countries and peoples of the world.

status quo: the existing state of affairs.

Membership

According to some critics, membership in the Security Council continues to reflect the world as it was in 1945, dominated by colonial rule. To these critics, the Security Council hasn't changed with **globalization** and the **decolonization** of the world. As a "nod" toward increasing UN membership (and at the pressure of those members), in 1965 the Security Council increased its membership from eleven to fifteen. However, the new members are elected members with two-year terms; they do not have veto power or a permanent seat on the council. More than sixty years after its creation, much of the power of the Security Council still rests with the P-5, the victors of World War II.

Membership reform has centered around two options. First, some have suggested that the membership of the Security Council be increased as a whole. There has been no increase since 1965, and supporters of

Brazil's National Congress building in its capital, Brasilia. As a large Latin American country with a growing economy, Brazil has been considered by some to be a candidate for permanent membership in the Security Council, should it expand.

Prime Minister Angela Merkel of Germany, right, and Prime Minister Taro Aso of Japan, at a press conference in Berlin in 2009. Both countries are members of the G-4 and have been suggested as additional permanent members of the UN Security Council.

reform, both within and outside the council, contend it's time to include more countries. Others feel that to increase the membership would make the Security Council too big to be effective. Among those nations being considered for membership on the Security Council are Brazil, Germany, India, and Nigeria.

The other membership reform option that has been discussed for many years deals with the P-5. The permanent members have a great deal of power on the Security Council. Because any one of them can veto an action, some critics claim it makes the Security Council "undemocratic and ineffective," as the veto can prevent issues from reaching the council's **agenda**. In some cases, just the threat of using the veto, called the closet veto, has influenced council actions.

Since 1946, the P-5 veto has been used 261 times. Most vetoes were cast between 1946 and 1995; 13 vetoes were cast between 1996 and 2005. Between 1946 and 2008, the Soviet Union/Russia used its veto power the most—124 times—with the United States next with 82 vetoes; in third place is Great Britain with 32 vetoes. Most of the recent vetoes have concerned proposals dealing with Israel and Palestine.

Representatives from India, Japan, Germany, and Brazil have joined forces to become the Group of Four—the G-4. They have agreed to support each other's bid to become a permanent member of the Security Council. The G-4 hopes their united stand will hasten Security Council membership reform and convince the council that one of them should have a new seat.

Also looking for representation as a permanent member of the Security Council is the African Union. The African Union was established with the goal of creating on the African continent an organization similar to the European Union. The organization insists that any expansion of the Security Council should include two permanent seats for countries from Africa—with veto power.

The P-5 is content with the **status quo**, and attempts to increase the number of permanent members have been turned away. In an attempt to reach a compromise, some have recommended that the number of permanent members be increased, but that new members not be given veto power.

Transparency

The only official meetings of the Security Council are public ones attended by the representatives of its member states. On three occasions since its founding, however, the Security Council has convened summit meetings on the head-of-state level. During these meetings, the heads of government represent their countries. For example, at the Security Council Summit on Threats to Peace and Security held in September 2005, President George W. Bush represented the United States. Records are kept and made public of these meetings.

HISTORIC MEETING

In 2009, Barak Obama became the first U.S. president to chair a Security Council meeting. He did so again in 2014 as he called on nations to stop the flow of foreign fighters into Iraq and Syria. It was only the sixth time a head of state chaired a meeting of the Security Council.

President Barack Obama chairing the UN Security Council meeting in September 2009, the first time a U.S. president was to do so.

Much of the time, however, the Security Council meets informally. These informal meetings can include the entire membership of the Security Council or as few as two people—two Security Council members or a council member and nonmember. Because it's informal, there is no requirement to release a record of these meetings, and they are not required to follow established procedures. Critics have rebuked the Security Council for the secrecy—the lack of transparency—that surrounds these informal consultations.

Much of the work of the Security Council takes place in these informal consultations. Some critics believe too much work is done away from public view, is not subject to official rules and regulations, and does not take advantage of the expertise of people outside of the United Nations. These critics are concerned that "backroom deals" could place the United Nations in an awkward position or place its work in jeopardy, or that the Security Council as a whole and the General Assembly will be asked to vote on something without knowing the full details.

The Security Council has taken steps to become more transparent, less secretive. More public meetings are being held, and experts have increasingly been allowed to present their opinions before the council. Meetings of the Security Council have moved outside the confines of UN headquarters in New York City to the locations of UN missions. Through this exposure, the Security Council gets a look at the real world—the one directly affected by its actions.

* * *

Despite criticisms from within and outside, the Security Council continues to work hard on behalf of world peace. And the members most responsible for fulfilling the Security Council's mandate are its permanent members.

CHAPTER THREE

TEXT-DEPENDENT QUESTIONS

1. How many member states are part of the Security Council?

2. Which country has used its veto the most?

3. Which nations are part of the G-4?

RESEARCH PROJECT

1. Create a bar chart comparing the number of vetoes by each P-5 member.

2. Create a fictional conflict somewhere in the world. Assign someone to be each member of the Security Council and representatives of the conflicting countries. Debate whether UN forces should get involved.

One of the permanent members of the Security Council, the United States has played an important role in the history of the United Nations.

CHAPTER FOUR

The United States and the Security Council

Just because the U.S. Congress refused to back President Woodrow Wilson and the League of Nations didn't mean that it felt such a peacekeeping organization wasn't necessary. Even before the United States entered into World War II, President Franklin D. Roosevelt was helping to plan an international organization that would be more effective than the League of Nations. In August 1941, he and British prime minister Winston Churchill met off the coast of Newfoundland at the Atlantic Conference. President Roosevelt and

WORDS TO UNDERSTAND

Great Depression: the drastic decline in the world economy resulting in mass unemployment and widespread poverty that lasted from 1929 until 1939.

ideals: standards or principles to which people aspire.

integral: being an essential part of something.

ironic: characterized by irony, where the actual result of a sequence of events and the normal or expected result do not match.

Prime Minister Churchill signed the Atlantic Charter, which outlined the postwar world order and the international organization that would replace the League of Nations. The president wanted the United States to have an **integral** role in the new "United Nations." As it had been at the beginning of World War I, the United States was officially neutral in this conflict. Then came Pearl Harbor.

"A Date Which Will Live in Infamy"

The late 1920s and 1930s were difficult years for the United States. The **Great Depression** spread across the country, hitting most those who could afford it the least. When conflict broke out in Europe, it was an opportunity for the U.S. economy to begin to grow. The government provided financial support and U.S.-made war material to the United Kingdom, the Soviet Union, and China, countries already in combat with Germany. But, President Roosevelt was not ready to send his country to war.

People's lives can change in an instant, and on December 7, 1941, the lives of every person in the United States were altered in a way few at that time could have anticipated. At 7:53 in the morning, the first wave of Japanese aircraft reached the island of Oahu, Hawaii. This first attack, carried out by 183 planes, surprised those on the U.S. carriers

Pictured here is the battleship USS *Arizona* sinking after the Japanese attack on Pearl Harbor on December 7, 1941. The surprise attack caused the United States to enter World War II on the side of the Allies.

and battleships and those stationed at air bases across Oahu. The 170 aircraft of the second wave of the Japanese attack struck a marine and naval base at Pearl Harbor. The next day, the U.S. Congress declared war on Japan. President Roosevelt signed the declaration of war, calling December 7 "a date which will live in infamy."

On December 11, Germany and Italy declared war on the United States, and U.S. forces prepared to return to war in Europe as a member of the Allies. The United Kingdom welcomed the addition of the United States into the conflict, making it a true world war. In his book *The Second World War*, Prime Minister Churchill wrote that after he heard the United States had entered the war, "Being saturated and satiated with emotion and sensation, I went to bed and slept the sleep of the saved and thankful."

Congresswoman Jeannette Rankin, from Montana, who said no to U.S. entrance into World War II.

A VOTE AGAINST WORLD WAR II

Jeannette Rankin of Montana was the first woman elected to Congress. She was also the only person to vote against going to war with Japan, saying "As a woman, I can't go to war, and I refuse to send anyone else."

A World Leader

Even while war raged in Europe and Asia, representatives of the Allies worked to put together an effective organization to help the world pick up the pieces when the latest conflict ended. Not long after the United States entered the war, it joined the Soviet Union, the United Kingdom, and China to formalize the proposals President Roosevelt and Prime Minister Churchill had agreed on in the Atlantic Charter. Meetings continued throughout the course of the war, with the United States taking the lead, until the United Nations was established in 1945.

Since its inception, the United States has been a driving force on the Security Council. The United States has used its veto powers more than eighty-two times since 1946, mostly in resolutions condemning actions by the state of Israel. U.S. support of Israel's actions has caused friction between the General Assembly, which has frequently condemned the government of Israel, and the Security Council, which has not because of the U.S. veto.

A staunch supporter of Israel, the United States often uses its veto power in the Security Council when issues arise relating to the conflict between Israel and Palestine. Pictured here is the Israel Defense Force circa 1950, three years after the UN General Assembly voted in favor of a partition plan that established the state of Israel.

FLEXING U.S. MUSCLE

Beginning in 2001 and ending in 2014, the United States used its veto the most of any P-5 member: twelve times. By contrast, Russia used its veto nine times and China five times. Almost all of the U.S. vetoes involved questions concerning Israel and the Palestinians. The following is a list of U.S. vetoes from March 2001 to December 2014:

December 30, 2014
Middle East situation, including the Palestinian question

February 18, 2011
Middle East situation, including the Palestinian question

November 11, 2006
Middle East situation, including the Palestinian question

July 13, 2006
Middle East situation, including the Palestinian question

October 5, 2004
Middle East situation, including the Palestinian question

March 25, 2004
Middle East situation, including the Palestinian question

October 14, 2003
The situation in the Middle East, including the Palestinian question

September 16, 2003
The situation in the Middle East, including the Palestinian question

December 20, 2002
The situation in the Middle East, including the Palestinian question

June 30, 2002
The situation in Bosnia and Herzegovina

December 14-15, 2001
The situation in the Middle East, including the Palestinian question

March 27-28, 2001
The situation in the Middle East, including the Palestinian question

The world has changed much since the first meeting of the Security Council. The Soviet Union is no longer a superpower—it's not even the Soviet Union anymore—and the fear of nuclear annihilation of the 1950s and 1960s is gone; in schools, there are no more "duck-and-cover drills" held alongside fire drills. As the only remaining world superpower, the United States arguably has more influence on the Security Council than the other members of the P-5. That doesn't mean, however, that the rest of the United Nations, or even the rest of the Security Council, always agrees with U.S. actions.

The Iraq War

At the end of the twentieth century, for example, the United States pushed for war against Iraq. It found, however, that not all members of the P-5 or Security Council were in favor of going to war. The Security Council, including the P-5, was split as to whether the United States should be authorized to invade Iraq and overthrow Saddam Hussein, the country's dictator.

The bombing of the UN headquarters in Baghdad during the Iraq War in 2003. Following the destruction, the UN removed its personnel.

In reaction to the United Nations not authorizing its invasion of Iraq, the United States limited UN influence over Iraq's affairs during the period after the fall of Baghdad. Then, in August 2003, the United Nations pulled out of the country completely after insurgents bombed its headquarters in Baghdad. However, growing Iraqi resistance to the U.S. military occupation prompted the United States to seek international support from the United Nations. Since the United Nations returned to Iraq in August 2004, it worked on the country's political transitions and advised the Iraqi constitution drafting committee.

In 2005, Iraq drafted a new constitution with the help of the UN. The UN also assisted in the process of reconstruction, promoting new development, providing humanitarian assistance, promoting and protecting human rights, and building a functional judicial system.

The U.S. began withdrawing from Iraq in December 2007, completing the mission in 2011. However, by the fall of 2014, a new terrorist threat emerged—ISIS, or ISIL. The group, known as the Islamic State in Iraq and Syria, emerged from the region and began a terrorist campaign across eastern Syria and northern and western Iraq. Although not sanctioned by the UN, the United States and several of its allies, including the British, began air strikes against ISIS in Iraq and in Syria.

EXPANDING THE SECURITY COUNCIL

Although the United States has indicated that it is not completely opposed to the expansion of the Security Council and the P-5, it has opposed Germany's bid for a permanent seat on the council. Some critics claim that the opposition stems from Germany's lack of support for the Iraq War. Meanwhile, Japan has U.S. backing for a permanent seat on the council, but without the veto power. Although it might seem **ironic** that either of the aggressors of World War II be given a seat on a council composed of the war's victors, it reflects the changing world of today.

U.S. military board an aircraft in Kuwait in 2006 on their way to Baghdad, Iraq, during the U.S.-led Iraq War.

U.S. Attitudes Toward Reform

The United States relationship to reforming the Security Council is complex. As for increased its transparency, the United States generally sides with the other P-5 members in vetoing changes to the council's working methods. They have allowed more public meetings.

While the council and the United Nations do work more closely with nongovernmental organizations, much of their work remains secret. Some critics claim that this resistance to change is spearheaded by U.S. representatives.

Is There Room for a Superpower in a United World?

The very design of the United Nations does not encourage a world dominated by a single nation; rather, the UN's **ideals** are based on all nations working together as equals. Although the P-5 nations have always held more power than the other UN members, so long as the Soviet Union's power was equal to that of the United States, America's influence was counterbalanced. After the fall of the Soviet Union in 1991, this was no longer the case. Because of the U.S. military conflicts in the Middle East, many nations would like to use the United Nations as a vehicle to rein in America. Meanwhile, the United States has sought to limit the UN's power over it.

Conflict between the United States and the United Nations is not new. The first major American defeat within the United Nations was in 1971 with Resolution 2758, the admission of the People's Republic of China to the United Nations and the removal of Taiwan, also known as the Republic of China.

CHAPTER FOUR

TEXT-DEPENDENT QUESTIONS

1. Who uttered the phrase "a date which will live in infamy" and to what does it refer?

2. Who was the only member of Congress to vote against a declaration of war against Japan in World War II?

3. What was the involvement of the United Nations in the Iraq War?

RESEARCH PROJECTS

1. Research and write a report about the relationship between Winston Churchill and Franklin Roosevelt during World War II.

2. Research and write a report about the Security Council's work on the Iraq War.

The flag of China, with the Great Wall in the background.

CHAPTER FIVE

China and the Security Council

The Republic of China and Japan had been at war since July 7, 1937, after the Marco Polo Bridge Incident near present-day Beijing. An **allegedly** unplanned fight took place there between China and Japan, which escalated into the Second Sino-Japanese War. That war, and Japan's attempt to gain control over much of Asia, continued throughout World War II, not ending until Japan's surrender in 1945 at the hands of the Allies.

 WORDS TO UNDERSTAND

allegedly: not yet proven.

atrocities: shockingly cruel acts, especially against an enemy during wartime.

Cold War: a hostile, largely nonviolent conflict between capitalist and communist countries following the end of World War II.

scorched-earth: describing a military policy involving deliberate and widespread destruction of property and resources.

theater: a place where significant events take place especially in wartime.

In many respects, the Chinese army was no match for Japanese forces. China's military leaders adopted a **scorched-earth** policy to hold off the Japanese until it had enough foreign aid to fight Japan's army. The quality and loyalty of China's troops was uneven from unit to unit. Many of the units were untrained. The Chinese people suffered many **atrocities** during this time as well, including slavery and torture.

Although China and Japan had been fighting for many years before the attack on the United States at Pearl Harbor, China did not declare war on Japan until December 8, 1941, the day after Japan's attack. Before that, some of the countries providing aid to China, including the United States, were neutral, and China was afraid that to declare war on Japan would compromise the donor countries' neutrality—and their support of the China effort.

Shortly after the attack on Pearl Harbor, the United States established military operations in China, often referred to as the U.S. China-Burma-India **theater**. The Allies, especially U.S. forces, carried out most of the

A column of Chinese soldiers in 1943 during World War II on the Salween River front in the western part of the country.

DYNAMIC CHINA

China is one of the world's oldest civilizations and one of its most dynamic. Its modern history began when Sun Yet-sen came to power in 1911. At the time, he did away with China's monarchy and feudal system. He established the Republic of China and guided his country down the road of modernization.

Chiang Ka-shek succeeded Sun and became increasingly intolerant and dictatorial as he sought to modernize China in the mold of liberal Western societies. After Sun's death, Chiang cooperated with the Communists to conquer warlords and capture Beijing. Then Chiang turned against the Communists and sent troops to fight them. The Communists, led by Mao Zedong, retreated during the Long March, but they won peasant support by redistributing land.

fighting in China. Getting troops and supplies to China was not easy, as they had to be shipped over long distances to India and then transported to China, or flown over the treacherous Himalayas.

Another complication in the war effort was confusion over who was in charge of the Chinese forces. Generalissimo Chiang Kai-shek was the Allied Supreme Commander, China Theater. However, U.S. generals served as his chiefs of staff, directing much of the military effort. After initial difficulties, including some caused by the extreme cultural differences, China did its part in the defeat of the Axis powers in World War II, preventing many Japanese troops from being sent to the Pacific. As a result, China became a founding member of the United Nations and the holder of a permanent seat on the Security Council.

China on the Security Council

China's membership in the United Nations and on the Security Council has not been without controversy. When the United Nations and the Security Council were formed in 1945, the seat was held by the Republic of China. Four years later, the Communist Party took control of mainland China and declared that the People's Republic of China was the country's only legitimate government.

Shanghai is one of the most populous cities in China, and its skyline shows that the country is taking its place in the modern world.

WHAT ABOUT THE REPUBLIC OF CHINA?

The Republic of China continues to function as the government of Taiwan. For more than fifteen years, it has expressed a desire to rejoin the United Nations. Each year its supporters attempt to place the matter on the agenda, and each year it fails. There is hope, however. If the Republic of China agrees to renounce its claim to being the legitimate government of mainland China and outer Mongolia, and if it changes its name to the Republic of Taiwan, some feel that the new country could apply and be accepted for membership in the United Nations. Many doubt this will happen, as the international community recognizes the People's Republic of China's claim that Taiwan is a province of China.

The former government was left to rule on the island of Taiwan, though it also claimed to be the only legitimate government of the mainland. During the 1950s and 1960s, the United States and others on the Security Council and General Assembly agreed. This was the time of the **Cold War** and they did not want another communist country to hold a permanent seat on the Security Council. The Soviet Union, a member of the P-5 and a communist ally of the People's Republic of China, boycotted the United Nations from January to August 1950. During its absence from the Security Council and the United Nations, UN troop deployments to Korea were approved.

Conflict between the Republic of China and the Soviet Union continued in 1952. China filed a complaint with the United Nations against the Soviet Union, alleging that it had violated the Sino-Soviet Treaty of Friendship and Alliance as well as the UN Charter. The General Assembly found in favor of the Republic of China, and the Soviet Union was condemned for its actions.

Beginning in the early 1960s, the General Assembly could expect a yearly proposal by supporters of the People's Republic of China to transfer China's membership to that government. U.S.-led opposition defeated each resolution. This yearly routine changed, however, with the changing face of the United Nations. What was once a Western-dominated organization began to change during the early 1970s; third-world nations were gaining power. The U.S. government also wanted to improve its relationship with China. So, the U.S. delegation stopped its heavy campaigning to block the yearly resolution from the People's Republic of China for a status change. On October 25, 1971, the General Assembly passed the resolution acknowledging the People's Republic of China as the legitimate government of China. China's seat on the Security Council went to the representative of the People's Republic.

The People's Republic of China has used its veto only six times since it took China's seat. (The Republic of China had used its veto power once.) It has participated in peacekeeping missions by sending military observers and civilian police as part of UN forces to hot spots.

The Korean War was fought between UN troops in the south of the country, led by U.S. forces, and the Communist forces in the North of the country. Following the end of the conflict in 1953, the country was divided into the Communist North Korea and western-allied South Korea.

China's economic influence becomes stronger every day, which helps to increase its global political power, reflected in its activity on the UN Security Council.

China and UN Reforms

The People's Republic of China supports the expansion of the Security Council. In 2004, Chinese Foreign Ministry spokesperson Zhang Qiyue stated that though China agrees that the council should be expanded to reflect the changing times and membership of the United Nations, "the expansion should proceed through broad discussions and consultations of all of the UN members." China also supports the addition of Germany as a permanent member of the UN Security Council.

It also favors changing some of the working methods of the Security Council as well. In particular, it supports the use of nonmembers, especially nongovernmental organizations, more often. Though China believes that holding more public meetings might be advantageous, it needs more consideration before a decision is made.

CHINA AND PEACEKEEPING

Over the years, China has contributed 20,000 troops to various UN peacekeeping missions. Currently, China is the largest troop-contributing country among the permanent members of the Security Council with more than 2,000 peacekeepers serving in ten peacekeeping operations. Chinese peacekeepers are in Mali and South Sudan.

CHAPTER FIVE

TEXT-DEPENDENT QUESTIONS

1. Who was Chiang Kai-shek and why was he important?

2. Why did the Soviet Union boycott the United Nations from January to August 1950?

3. Which year did the communists take over China?

RESEARCH PROJECTS

1. Describe in a brief essay the conflict between the People's Republic of China and Taiwan.

2. Break into groups and create a list of countries you think should sit on the Security Council. Hold a debate with your classmates stating your reasons why these nations should be on the council.

From left to right, Soviet Union premier Joseph Stalin, U.S. president
Franklin Roosevelt, and British prime minister Winston Churchill—
leaders of the Allied forces during World War II, meeting in Tehran in
1943, at the Russian Embassy.

CHAPTER SIX

France, Russia, the United Kingdom, and the Security Council

The other three members of the Security Council—France, Russia, and the United Kingdom—also gained their places on the Security Council because of their roles during World War II. Since the 1940s, each of these nations has undergone changes in its status, and yet all continue to be major world players who have maintained their roles as P-5 nations.

 WORDS TO UNDERSTAND

exile: unwilling absence from one's home country.

steppe: a level and treeless tract of land.

subtext: an underlying meaning or message.

U-boats: German submarines used during World War II.

unanimously: done with complete agreement.

France

After Germany invaded Poland in 1939, France declared war on the aggressor nation. A year later, Germany invaded France and occupied the country until the Allies liberated it in 1944.

World War I had devastated France, and self-protection was France's prime goal in the years after the war. The French people did not want a repetition of the massive property destruction and loss of life that had resulted from World War I. In an attempt to save their rebuilt industrial areas, France constructed the Maginot Line, stretching from Switzerland to the Ardennes in northeastern France. The line was made of concrete fortifications, tank obstacles, machine gun posts, and other defenses. Experts believed the German army could not cross the rough terrain of the Ardennes. They were wrong.

On May 9 and 10, 1940, German forces attacked and occupied Luxembourg, and then attacked Belgium and Holland. While British and French military forces countered those battles, other German forces went after the real target, France. To get there, they went through the Ardennes. The German Luftwaffe, air forces, easily defeated the French and British air divisions. The expensive Maginot Line didn't provide the level of protection the French had hoped it would. The German forces were too strong and too fast for the French and the British troops.

The French government moved its headquarters from Paris to Tours on June 12. British prime minister Winston Churchill met with French officials in Tours. The British government was concerned that France would give up, leaving Britain to fight on its own. Churchill suggested that France and Britain form a single state, but the French government refused. His mission a failure, Prime Minister Churchill returned to Britain. On June 14, the French government moved to Bordeaux.

After discussion about moving the government to French colonies in North Africa and continuing to battle Germany, the French government took the suggestion of World War I hero Marshal Philippe Pétain and surrendered to Germany on June 24, 1940. By then, Germany occupied three-fifths of France. The Germans established a new government on

The flag of the French Republic, with Paris's Arc de Triomphe in the background.

July 10, 1940, in Vichy, headed by Marshal Philippe Pétain. Some members of the government aided the Germans in stealing from the French and sending their citizens to labor camps in Germany. Civilians and government officials participated in persecution of France's Jewish population.

Not all of France was ready to give in to the Germans, however. Civilian activists went underground in the Resistance struggle against Nazi forces, and the Free French Forces, under the leadership of future president Charles de Gaulle, formed in **exile** with the support of the United Kingdom.

U.S. troops discuss strategy with Resistance fighters during the Normandy invasion in the summer of 1944, when the Allies liberated France from Nazi occupation.

Together with the Allied forces, the Free French Forces liberated France in 1944. When the United Nations formed the next year, this war-ravaged country, as a member of the Allied forces, became a permanent member of the Security Council.

France has sometimes been very outspoken on issues it disagrees with when they come before the UN Security Council. Since its inception, France has used its veto only eighteen times. But it has threatened to use its veto power more, most recently concerning resolutions dealing with the war in Iraq. The French were concerned with what they saw as a "rush to war" on the part of the United States and other members of the Security Council. French foreign minister Dominique de Villepin insisted that "war in Iraq would only worsen tensions and the sense of injustice and, consequently, the risk of terrorism and violence." The war resolution never went before the Security Council, so France did not have to use its veto power.

Of all the permanent members of the Security Council, France is one of the few to have found the validity of its position questioned. Both Israel and Italy have stated that France should be replaced on the Security Council. According to a 2005 article in the *Italian Voice*, Italy should replace France

FRANCE, THE UNITED STATES, and THE SECURITY COUNCIL

The Iraq conflict is not the first time France and the United States have gone toe-to-toe over a Security Council issue. The first time was the Suez Canal crisis in 1956. France and Britain used their vetoes for the first time to block a resolution calling for Israel to withdraw from territory it had seized from Egypt. France and Britain also blocked resolutions for a cease-fire. U.S. president Dwight Eisenhower was so angry over their actions that he took the matter before the General Assembly, but the veto power does not work at the General Assembly. The assembly passed the resolution demanding that all parties withdraw, and a UN peacekeeping force was formed for the first time.

as a permanent member of the Security Council. It reminds readers that France surrendered to Germany. In a 2003 article in the *Jerusalem Post*, Shimon Peres criticizes France for its opposition to the U.S. position on the Iraq War and wonders aloud why it still has a veto power. It is unlikely that France will be removed as a permanent member with veto power, however.

On reforming the Security Council, France agrees that it should be enlarged and backs Japan's efforts to obtain a permanent seat. It also supports efforts by Germany, Brazil, India, and the African Union to become permanent members of the Security Council. As do most permanent members of the Security Council, France is in favor of reforming the council's meeting methods, including consultations with more experts and nongovernmental organizations.

FRENCH PROPOSAL

In 2013, France proposed a "code of conduct" that would limit the use of the veto in the Security Council in situations of genocide, war crimes, and crimes against humanity. At the time, France had been frustrated by the Security Council's inaction in the Syrian Civil War. The French proposed that P-5 members suspend the veto in cases of war crimes and other atrocities. It would be up to the Security Council, if at least fifty member states agreed, to determine the nature of the crimes. Once that occurred, the code of conduct would immediately apply.

A Russian flag flying over the Kremlin.

Russia

Before World War II, in an attempt to avoid conflict, the Soviet Union signed a nonaggression treaty with Germany. Unfortunately, this meant that as it honored the treaty, it was forced to stand by as Germany invaded Poland. Then, on June 22, 1941, Germany invaded the Soviet Union. Surprise attacks destroyed much of the Soviet military force in the west. Hundreds of thousands of men were killed or captured. Soviet forces withdrew to Russia's **steppe** to gain time in their fight against the German troops. Germany vowed to capture Moscow, but when German troops were delayed by winter weather, Soviet forces were able to defeat them, just short of Germany's goal of Moscow. Though Soviet forces were stretched thin, they were able to take advantage of their knowledge of Soviet winters and defeat Axis powers in many areas of the country.

In February 1945, the United Kingdom's Winston Churchill, the Soviet Union's Joseph Stalin, and America's Franklin Roosevelt met in the resort town of Yalta in the Soviet Union. The purpose of the meeting was to hammer out arrangements for postwar Europe. How to deal with the Soviet Union was a definite **subtext** of the meeting, and Churchill and Roosevelt were uncertain about the Soviet Union's motives. One of the resolutions of the conference was that the Soviet Union would attack Japan within three months of Germany's surrender. On August 8, 1945, the Soviet Union declared war on Japan, as it had promised to do at Yalta. A week later, August 15, 1945, Japan surrendered.

According to some reports, of the almost 62 million people who lost their lives as a result of World War II, about half were Russians. These figures include military and civilians.

Following the war, getting the Soviet Union to participate in the formation of the new United Nations was a major purpose of the Yalta Conference. Stalin agreed to this as long as each permanent member of the Security Council received the veto power and that any alterations to the UN Charter be **unanimously** approved first by the five permanent members of the Security Council. It was agreed, and the Soviet Union's participation was

A demonstration at a tank factory in Great Britain in honor of the Soviet ambassador to Britain and members of the Soviet military mission, around 1942. That week, the factory was producing tanks destined for use by the Russian military in its offensive against German forces.

guaranteed. There had been another requirement, though: Stalin also wanted each of the Soviet Union's republics to be recognized by the United Nations as nations. When the United States said that it then wanted all forty-eight states (Alaska and Hawaii were not yet states) to be recognized as independent nations, Stalin withdrew that requirement.

In 1950, the Soviet Union boycotted the United Nations in protest of the refusal to designate the People's Republic of China as that country's official representative. During that time, the Security Council authorized the Korean War, a resolution that might have been vetoed had the Soviet Union been in attendance.

When the Soviet Union retook its seat on the UN Security Council later that same year, it marked the beginning of a period of active participation. The Soviet Union has exercised its veto more than any other permanent member—124 times since 1945. Since 1995, however, Russia has used its veto three times. During the first years of the United Nations, the Soviet representative to the council voted no so many times he was called "Mr. Veto."

When the Soviet Union dissolved in 1991, the new government informed the United Nations that the Russian Federation would be its successor on the Security Council. Unlike the China case, there was no conflict over which government was the country's legitimate representative.

In reference to reforms, Russia has indicated that it will support a limited expansion of the UN Security Council. In 2000, Foreign Minister Igor Ivanov stated: "The composition of the reformed Security Council should be balanced to the utmost: along with industrialized countries, it should contain major influential developing countries pursuing independent foreign policies." He went on to state that there should not be a time limit set on expanding the Security Council.

The flag of the United Kingdom flying in London at the Palace of Westminster, the seat of the British Parliament.

The United Kingdom

World War I had been hard on the United Kingdom, but when Germany invaded Poland, the United Kingdom did not hesitate to enter into the fray that would become World War II. When conflict first began, the Allies consisted of the United Kingdom and France, each with their empires. Both declared war on Germany on September 3, 1939, in response to the German invasion of Poland. British troops were apparently caught off-guard when Germany attacked Poland.

Germany believed it would be able to achieve a quick peace with Britain, but that was not to be. So Germany began the planning of the Battle of Britain, an air battle between the Luftwaffe and the Royal Air Force (RAF). Though Germany initially targeted the RAF Fighter Command, its attention quickly turned to the city of London. Night after night,

FAMOUS WORDS

One of the most memorable quotes of World War II came from British prime minister Winston Churchill. Spoken to the British Parliament on June 4, 1940, he said:

We shall defend our island, whatever the cost may be, we shall fight on the beaches, we shall fight on the landing grounds, we shall fight in the fields and in the streets, we shall fight in the hills; we shall never surrender.

the city was the target of bombs dropping like rain. Air raid sirens were an every-night occurrence, and air raid wardens walked the streets to make certain that all windows were covered and no light from within the buildings could be seen. Despite the terror caused by the bombings, the city and its people could not be defeated.

Germany also attempted to thwart the United Kingdom's war efforts by using **U-boats** to attack sea cargo coming into the country. Though the shipments were reduced, the United Kingdom and Prime Minister Winston Churchill refused to approach the Germans asking for peace.

On December 7, 1941, Japanese forces attacked U.S. bases in Pearl Harbor, then went on to invade the British colonies of Hong Kong, Malaya, Borneo, and Burma. But December 7 also brought the United States into the war.

The United Kingdom fought in Africa as well, as its empire was extensive. In 1942, Field Marshall Bernard Montgomery won a hard-fought battle, giving Allied forces a staging area. The battle had been hard on equipment, however; his forces lost more tanks than Germany had when the battle began.

Late in the war, in February 1945, and amid much controversy, the RAF and the U.S. Air Force bombed the city of Dresden. Although the exact number of civilians who died in the bombing is unknown, it is estimated that tens of thousands lost their lives in the Allied attack.

Also in February 1945, Prime Minister Winston Churchill met with Joseph Stalin and Franklin Roosevelt at the Yalta Conference to plan the postwar world. When Japan signed the official surrender papers on September 2, 1945, the war was over, and the plans devised by the three world leaders could be put into action.

WHAT EXACTLY IS THE UNITED KINGDOM?

The United Kingdom is made up of several individual countries that can act on their own with some autonomy. These include:

- England
- Scotland
- Northern Ireland
- Wales

On matters of foreign policy, international trade regulations, and other issues of critical importance, the United Kingdom operates as one country.

The Allied war effort worked on a global scale during World War II. Pictured here is a plant in Malaya, then a British colony (which later become Malaysia), where U.S.-made aircraft were assembled for the use of Britain's Royal Air Force in East Asia.

The UK was a major player in the UN from the beginning. It has used its veto on the Security Council thirty-two times since 1945; it hasn't vetoed any actions since 1995. In all but nine times, the United States also cast a veto for the same issue. (In seven cases the resolutions concerned South Rhodesia, present-day Zimbabwe, and the other two were against Israeli actions.) The United Kingdom's closeness to the United States has brought some criticism. Just as some people suspect France opposes much that the United States favors, others consider that the United Kingdom is walking in lockstep with U.S. policies.

The United Kingdom has been active in the UN reform movement and is a member of the Open Ended Working Group on Security Council Reform. The United Kingdom has publicly supported the expansion of the Security

Council, including permanent and nonpermanent members. It supports permanent membership for Germany, Japan, India, and Brazil, as well as a representative from an African nation. Increased transparency is also advocated by the United Kingdom. It particularly supports the increased involvement of nonmembers and the use of consultants.

* * *

When the United Nations was established in 1945, the founders could have had little idea how much the world would change by the turn of the century. As the world changes, power shifts, and goals change, the United Nations and the Security Council will have to adapt to remain relevant. Change is difficult and oftentimes slow, but with world peace at stake, it's worth the effort.

The close relationship of the United States and the UK, especially as it plays out on the UN Security Council, is well-known. Pictured here is U.S. president Barack Obama and UK prime minister Gordon Brown conferring during a session of the UN Security Council in September of 2009.

CHAPTER SIX

TEXT-DEPENDENT QUESTIONS

1. Describe the antagonism that sometimes exists between the United States and France on the Security Council.

2. Why did Roosevelt, Stalin, and Churchill meet at Yalta?

3. Describe the relationship between the United States and Great Britain on the Security Council.

RESEARCH PROJECTS

1. Choose the votes of the five members of the UN Security Council and research their record of votes over the last three years. Make a chart comparing them all.

2. Hold a mock Security Council debate on an issue of importance today. The issue should be outlined in a "resolution" that calls for action. Pick five delegates who represent the five permanent members of the Security Council, and four or five others who represent other council members. Each member should research the issue, form an opinion, and then debate the resolution.

TIME LINE

1920	The Treaty of Versailles is ratified.
September 3, 1939	France and the United Kingdom declare war on Germany following Germany's invasion of Poland.
May 9–10, 1940	Germany attacks France; France surrenders on June 24.
June 22, 1941	Germany invades the Soviet Union.
August 1941	President Franklin Roosevelt and Prime Minister Winston Churchill meet at the Atlantic Conference.
December 7, 1941	Japanese planes attack U.S. bases in Pearl Harbor, Hawaii, which leads to the U.S. entry into World War II on the side of the Allies.
January 1, 1942	The term "United Nations" is used in reference to a worldwide organization for the first time.
1944	The Allies liberate France.
August–October 1944	Representatives meet at Dumbarton Oaks to work out details of the United Nations.
February 1945	The Yalta Conference between the United States, the United Kingdom, and the Soviet Union meets.
February 1945	The RAF and U.S. Air Force bomb Dresden.
August 8, 1945	The Soviet Union declares war on Japan.
August 15, 1945	Japan surrenders.

April 1945	The United Nations Conference on International Organization meets in San Francisco.
June 26, 1945	The UN Charter is signed.
January–August 1950	The Soviet Union boycotts the United Nations.
1952	The Republic of China files a complaint with the United Nations against the Soviet Union.
1956	The Suez Canal crisis pits France and Britain against the United States in the Security Council.
1963	Geographical distribution of elected members of the Security Council is passed.
1965	Article 23 of the UN Charter is passed, increasing membership in the Security Council to fifteen.
October 25, 1971	The UN General Assembly passes a resolution acknowledging the People's Republic of China as the legitimate government of China.
1991	The Soviet Union is dissolved, with the Russian Federation becoming the new government.
October 15, 1999	Security Council passes Resolution 1267, the first resolution dealing with al Qaeda.
September 11, 2001	The United States is attacked by al Qaeda terrorists.
August 2003	The United Nations pulls out of Iraq after its headquarters is attacked; it returns a year later.
September 2009	U.S. president Barack Obama chairs a meeting of the Security Council, the first time a U.S. president would do so.

FURTHER RESEARCH

Books

Basic Facts About the United Nations. New York: United Nations Publications, 2014.

Gaston, Erica. *Laws of War and 21st Century Conflict*. New York: International Debate Association, 2012.

Hanhimäki, Jussi M. *The United Nations: A Very Short Introduction*. New York: Oxford University Press, 2008.

Roberts, Priscilla. *World War II: The Essential Reference Guide*. Santa Barbara, CA: ABC-CLIO, 2012.

Online Sources

60th Anniversary of the San Francisco Conference
www.un.org/aboutun/sanfrancisco

The Avalon Project's World War II Documents Page
www.yale.edu/lawweb/avalon/wwii/yalta.htm

Global Policy Forum: www.globalpolicy.org/security/index.htm

United Nations Security Council: www.un.org/en/sc/

UN Security Council Resolutions
www.un.org/en/sc/documents/resolutions/

NOTE TO EDUCATORS: This book contains both imperial and metric measurements as well as references to global practices and trends in an effort to encourage the student to gain a worldly perspective. We, as publishers, feel it's our role to give young adults the tools they need to thrive in a global society.

SERIES GLOSSARY

abstain: not to vote for or against proposal when a vote is held.

Allies: the countries that fought against Germany in World War I or against the Axis powers in World War II.

ambassador: an official representative of one country to another country.

amendments: process of changing a legal document.

appeal: a formal request to a higher authority requesting a change of a decision.

appeasement: a deliberate attempt pacify a potentially troublesome nation.

arbitration: the process of resolving disputes through an impartial third party.

asylum: protection granted by a nation to someone who has left fled their country as a political refugee.

Axis: the alliance of Germany, Italy, and Japan that fought the allies in World War II.

blocs: groups of countries or political parties with the same goal.

bureaucracy: a complex system of administration, usually of a government or corporation.

capital: material wealth in the form of money or property.

civil law: law of a state dealing with the rights of private citizens.

coalition: in military terms, a group of nations joined together for a common purpose against a common enemy.

codification: the arrangement of laws into a systematic code.

Cold War: a largely nonviolent conflict between capitalist and communist countries following World War II.

compliance: conforming to a regulation or law.

conservation: preservation, management, and care of natural and cultural resources.

constitution: an official document outlining the rules of a system or government.

conventions: agreements between countries, less formal than treaties.

decolonization: the act of granting a colony its independence.

delegates: individuals chosen to represent or act on behalf of an organization or government.

demographic: characteristics of a human population.

diplomatic: having to do with international negotiations without resorting to violence.

disarmament: the reduction of a nation's supply of weapons or strength of its armed forces.

due process: the official procedures in legal cases required by law to ensure that the rights of all people involves are protected.

embargo: a government order limiting or prohibiting trade.

envoys: diplomats who act on behalf of a national government.

epidemic: a widespread occurrence of an infectious disease.

ethnic cleansing: the killing or imprisonment of an ethnic minority by a dominant group.

exchange rates: rates at which money of one country is exchanged the money of another.

extradition: the handing over by one government of someone accused of a crime in a different country for trial or punishment.

extremist: having to do with radical political or religious beliefs.

factions: smaller groups within larger groups that have opposing ideas.

fascist: relating to a system of government characterized by dictatorship, repression of opposition, and extreme nationalism.

flashpoints: areas of intense conflict and insecurity that often erupt into violent confrontation.

forgery: the act of making or producing an illegal copy of something.

free-market economy: economic system in which businesses operate without government control in matters such as pricing and wage levels.

genocide: systematic killing of all people from a national, ethnic, or religious group, or an attempt to do so.

globalization: the various processes that increase connections peoples of the world.

gross domestic product: total value of all goods and services produced within a country.

guerrilla: unorganized and small-scale warfare carried out by independent units.

human trafficking: the practice of seizing people against their will for the purpose of "selling" them for work, usually in the sex trade.

humanitarian: being concerned with or wanting to promote the well-being of other humans.

ideological: based on a specific system of beliefs, values, and ideas forming the basis of a social, economic, or political philosophy

indigenous: relating to the original inhabitants of an area or environment.

infrastructure: physical structures of a region, made up of roads, bridges, and so forth.

isolationism: the belief that a country should limit their involvement in the affairs of other countries.

mandate: an official instruction by an authority.

mediation: the process of resolving a dispute.

money laundering: the transferring of illegally obtained money through various businesses and accounts so as to hide it.

nationalists: people with an extreme sense of loyalty to their country.

nationalize: takeover by a government of a private business.

pandemic: a widespread epidemic in which a disease spreads to many countries and regions of the world.

per capita income: average amount earned by each individual in a country.

preamble: introduction, or opening words of a document.

precedent: established practice; a decision used as the basis of future decisions.

proliferation: the rapid spread of something.

propaganda: information or publicity put out by an organization or government to spread and promote a policy or idea.

protocols: preliminary memoranda often formulated and signed by diplomatic negotiators.

rapporteur: an official in charge of investigating and reporting to an agency, institution, or other entity.

ratification: the act of formally approving something.

referendum: a vote of the entire electorate on a question or questions put before it by the government or similar body.

reparation: compensation made by a nation defeated by others in a war.

sanction: a punishment imposed as a result of breaking a rule or law.

signatories: persons or governments who have signed a treaty and are bound by it.

sovereignty: self-rule, usually of a nation.

standard of living: the minimum amount of necessities essential to maintaining a comfortable life.

summit: a meeting between heads of government or other high-ranking officials.

sustainable: able to be maintained so that the resource is not depleted or damaged.

veto: the power of a person, country, or branch of government to reject the legislation of another.

INDEX

PICTURE CREDITS

BIOGRAPHIES

Author

IDA WALKER is a graduate of the University of Northern Iowa in Cedar Falls and did graduate work at Syracuse University in Syracuse, New York. She lives in upstate New York.

Series Advisor

BRUCE RUSSETT is Dean Acheson Professor of Political Science at Yale University and editor of the Journal of Conflict Resolution. He has taught or researched at Columbia, Harvard, M.I.T., Michigan, and North Carolina in the United States, and educational institutions in Belgium, Britain, Israel, Japan, and the Netherlands. He has been president of the International Studies Association and the Peace Science Society, and holds an honorary doctorate from Uppsala University in Sweden. He was principal adviser to the U.S. Catholic Bishops for their pastoral letter on nuclear deterrence in 1985, and codirected the staff for the 1995 Ford Foundation report, *The United Nations in Its Second Half Century*. He has served as editor of the *Journal of Conflict Resolution* since 1973. The twenty-five books he has published include *The Once and Future Security Council* (1997), *Triangulating Peace: Democracy, Interdependence, and International Organizations* (2001), *World Politics: The Menu for Choice* (8th edition 2006), and *Purpose and Policy in the Global Community* (2006).

Per RFP 03764 Follett School Solutions guarantees
hardcover bindings through SY 2024-2025
877.899.8550 or customerservice@follett.com